SABISHI
poems from japan

Wick Poetry Chapbook Series
Maggie Anderson, Editor

White Sustenance
Kat Snider Blackbird

Sleepwalking with Mayakovsky
Robert Brown

Sabishi: poems from japan
David Hassler

Rooms by the Sea
Mary Ann Samyn

SABISHI
poems from japan

David Hassler

The Kent State University Press

Kent, Ohio, & London, England

© 1994 by David Hassler
All rights reserved.
Library of Congress Catalog Card Number 94-26870
ISBN 0-87338-513-6
Manufactured in the United States of America

06 05 04 03 02 01 00 99   5 4 3

The Wick Poetry Chapbook Series is sponsored by the
Stan and Tom Wick Poetry Program and the Department
of English at Kent State University.

LIBRARY OF CONGRESS CATALOGING-IN-PUBLICATION DATA
Hassler, David 1964–
    Sabishi: poems from Japan / David Hassler.
        p.   cm. — (Wick poetry chapbook series)
    ISBN 0-87338-513-6 (pbk.: alk. paper) ∞
    1. Japan—Poetry. I. Title. II. Series.
PS3558.A7258S23 1994
811'.54—dc20   94-26870

British Library Cataloging-in-Publication data are available.

CONTENTS

ACKNOWLEDGMENTS

"Eating Soba" first appeared in 5 *AM* 7 (Fall 1994) and is reprinted with permission. I would like to thank Sharona Ben-Tov for her careful readings and encouragement, my friends James and Pauline Thornton, and Maggie Anderson for her patience and vision.

O - B O N

In sweltering August, on the last night
of o-bon, the three-day festival for the dead,
I arrive in the village of Komagome.
Families sit out at night on their front porches,
drinking tea or sake and tasting sweets,
wearing those cotton robes they slip into
after bathing—bright, loose yukatas.
Doors are left wide: orange paper lanterns
flicker to light the way for the dead,
who are invited to return to their homes.
Tables are set with their favorite foods
and flowers, instruments and books laid out
that they might want to use again.

On the first day the families went to meet
the souls of the dead at the water's edge,
and tonight they will accompany them back.
Everyone is gathered in a small park,
the ground neatly raked. Lanterns hang
from trees and around a small wooden stage,
where women in kimonos dance slowly in a circle
to the music of drum and flute.
One summer I danced the polka
with my mother on a bandstand downtown
at the corner of Main and Water. We galloped
and spun as I held her hand, feeling the back
of the nylon dress she had sewn, white
with a little red and blue somewhere in it.
Here, the women lift their arms, appearing
only slightly from sleeves, where

plum blossoms and cranes drop softly away.
They turn their hands like fans and dance alone.

If I could I would find my mother's dress.
I would pick a bouquet of dandelions and place
the soft hearts of artichokes on clean,
shiny plates. I would put on the Mamas and the Papas
or Blood, Sweat and Tears; leave by the back door,
the house bright and open behind me,
and down to the river,
curving just beyond our yard,
to meet her at the water's edge.

A MAN PLAYS
THE SHAKUHACHI

He draws the low hollow notes
from the wells of his lungs,
like those Priests of Empty Nothing
who played the bamboo flute
and begged in old Edo.
His tongue flutters a soft haunting
melody of rising wings and mist,
called "Tenderness of Cranes."
His fingers lift and fall,
as he bows over his flute.

Men have listened to this music of rivers,
growing old and taciturn, bitter in the throat
as the taste of green tea. Paper lanterns
float on wood, the names of the dead
brushed on their sides.

Hearing this, I drop yen in his basket
and go down into Harajuku Station.

READING ON TRAINS

I do not know what they are reading.
The script falls down the page
like rain on windowpanes.
Heads bob as they read.
Hands turn the pages backwards
from last to first, as eyes
travel to the palm of the hand.

I want to let go of my language for awhile
to learn Kanji, which means "time."
The time it takes to learn anything:
The patience of standing shoulder
to shoulder in trains weaving
through the city, the names of stations
slowing down and speeding up.
The time it takes to learn grass writing,
waiting for the moment when the sosho brush
with quick, barely legible strokes
touches paper—wet black ink revealing
the rhythm of our hearts.

SABISHI

I'm drinking coffee in the Shibuya
subway station underneath Hachiko Square,
named after the faithful dog, who,
as the story goes, waited here
every evening for his master.
The day his master died at work,
Hachiko waited until the last train,
and then came back every night
for years, to sit in front of the station.
I have seen his large granite paws
marking the spot for rendezvous.

Below him, I'm pressed against
the vent of a loud air conditioner,
when two old women approach,
bent like cypress trees growing
in small trays. They watch me,
nodding and smiling to each other
and say, *Aah, sabishi des ne!*
I do not know their language well,
but I guess they ask if I am lonely.

I have left blue days in Ohio
to come here and be lonely, but
I cannot explain to these women why,
or what I think I have lost.
I cannot explain how I want to crawl
under the engine of my heart
and tighten nuts and bolts.
I cannot explain the mechanics of it,
why being lonely is work I want to do.
But I smile and reply yes, *Sabishi des,*
and hear doors slide open,
a soft recorded voice
announcing the station, *Shibuya.*

A NIGHT IN TOKYO

We drank warm rice wine,
ate beef tongue and kimchi
and laughed deep from our bellies.

Someone handed me a microphone
and wanted me to sing
"Home on the Range."

I followed the words on a screen,
visions of prairies and fields.
Each time we walked through alleys

the room we went into got smaller
until it seemed we had stepped behind a wall.
I danced with the woman who sat on the bar.

At four in the morning I felt I'd known
my friend forever. With his head against
my arm, he said, *I must go home.*

We pissed in the streets and stopped a taxi.
He told the driver where to go.
I remember someone singing "Country Roads."

And I could swear I saw a man on the sidewalk
in his bathrobe with a golf club
practicing his swing.

EATING SOBA

I speak your language when I eat—
the silence of steam and scent
rising to me; red pepper, ginger, and soy.
This bowl's heat in my hands.
I snap apart chopsticks,
break the yoke of the raw egg
they call Full Moon that drifts
in the center as though in a pond.
I pull the soba noodles to my mouth,
un-making their long strings
and hiss. This is the sound
of eating soba, sucking in air,
loud and energetic.
I hear wood rasp and tap
inside the bowls as they are drained
and clacked down on the counter empty.
Customers come and go through
the heat and steam of these small
kitchen shops, ordering soba,
soba o-kudasai!

I bow over your bowl
your body, your broth.
These are my hands that hold you.
This is the sound of my lips, warm
breathing you in
saying soba!

THE ART OF LIVING

According to tradition,
this little arched bridge
is rebuilt every thirty years.
Carp, patron saints of children,
dart slowly in all directions.

Behind me, I hear the clear, polished
words, brought out for a special
occasion, *Good afternoon.*
When I turn around, I meet a man,
of my father's age, who tells me
that he has lived in New Jersey
working for Sony, nearly thirty years,
and that sometimes in this country,
he feels like a stranger, too.

He brags about his daughter,
the fencing champion, who is expected
to come back every summer and stay
with her grandparents here, in Tokyo.
One weekend, when I meet her,
she tells me they're a drag—

I see her grandmother nag and jab
with her finger: she doesn't act Japanese.
Her grandfather shuffles through the house,
mumbling to himself. He pretends he cannot
hear his wife anymore. Everyday he goes out
to stand on the veranda to reach atop
the wooden fence that borders his yard,
where he keeps a row of bonzai.
With special tools he carefully pares
and props the old pines, transplanting them
from tray to tray, cutting the roots
that have grown too deep. He trains
these ancient trees in the art of living.

THREE MOTHERS

I watch from across the tracks
    this scene between three women
in a train that has not begun to move.

I imagine them to be mothers.
    Their children, old enough now
to be in school, are not with them,

that familiar weight off their bodies.
    And they have time in the afternoon
when the house is quiet, doing

household chores, managing the family
    finances, or this excursion today,
shopping perhaps, sharing news and gossip.

Will their children grow up to be successful?
    Have they begun to study for the entrance exam?
One of them does all the talking and makes

faces of surprise and scorn, while another
    exchanges nods of agreement.
But the third mother sits back,

and may not even be listening,
    though she tries not to show it.
I watch her closely and somehow feel attached.

Then the train starts up and lurches
    forward. Without their seeming to notice,
they are carried away.

Cherry blossoms are falling,
and you will ride home
after work, drunk in a taxi.
Cherry blossoms are falling,
while children are carried
on their mothers' backs
or in front against breasts.
Cherry blossoms are falling.
You lean over another table
for the mamasan, pouring businessmen
drinks and lighting their cigarettes.
White and blowsy,
cherry blossoms are falling,
as hostesses in slippered feet
scurry around low tables,
their toes springy on matted floors.
The city is a sewer of blossoms.
Everyone drunk in the afternoon
lying under branches on soggy ground.
Romance, one hour in a love hotel,
something untold.
Cherry blossoms are falling.
Someone steps in front of a taxi
and is tossed in the air.

SHARIF'S FISH STEW

The smell of fish floats
under the crack of my door.
Sharif is cooking his weekly stew.
He carries the scent of his spices
in his hands and hair, and they
will not leave the soles of his feet,
though he washes them before prayer.
I believe his stew makes him strong.
Perhaps Muhammed can smell
the faith of his followers.

Sharif, my friend, keeps his faith
on the roof of our boarding house,
where he rents a tin shack that rattles
in the rain. He prays there at dawn
before riding the trains two hours
outside of the city to work in a factory.
He calls me King David and says I should try
some of his stew. It will give me strength,
the strength he must have at night for the women.
We laugh loud like sultans and kings.

I would like to write a few lines
that could last a week like Sharif's stew,
that would fill the air of kitchens,
because I have no prayers
and no recipe for my faith—
a few lines that could
linger in my palms
and not be washed away.

FRIENDS IN ASIA

In Seoul, afraid to wander,
I step into Paris Baguette
off the boulevard. An old guy
in overalls comes through the doors.
He stands next to me at the counter
and smiles, then bursts out,
Where ya from? as I point
to my croissant. It turns out he's
from Minnesota, where he owns a farm
and sells seed. I welcome his loose-jowled
talk and familiar face. He tells me
business has been good, and now
he's traveling through Asia,
visiting friends—
Friends? Well no, friend.
Then a moment later, *I suppose friends.*

James tells us about
his correspondence classes
that will give him a degree

in hypnosis. His voice excited, dramatic,
he tries to hold our attention. Scott and Bill
sit in the smokers' corner, where nonsmokers

won't go. Staring over their coffees with blank
expressions and taking long drags, they look as if
they've just woken up in their suits and ties.

Then P.J. blusters in, pirouetting on his toes,
flapping his arms at his sides.
He complains that his new Cardin suit

has been crushed on the train, says
he doesn't know why he even bothers
to look good. Alan spots me

from across the room, comes over
and says, *Hello David H.* With pale,
puffy face and slicked-back hair, he

reminds me of some salesman. He makes
a point of calling everyone by their name tags.
We all keep an eye on the huge, orange clock

that hangs above Amanda, who furiously shuffles
through the shelves of student folders
that are supposed to be ordered alphabetically.

She wants to know who has taken Kimoko
or was she not put back where she should go.
Two minutes are left before it's time.

Everyone holds on to the blue books
we'll need to stay afloat.
I'm wondering again

about the power of suggestion.
Someone asks if "since"
is considered a preposition.

MORNING RIDE
ON THE YAMANOTE LINE

The conductor's voice
glides over the drowsy heads,
like a familiar hand
smoothing unruly hair.
A schoolgirl in uniform
falls asleep on my shoulder
as the train tilts and sways.
She has forgotten about her satchel,
what she is carrying to school,
and sleeps in this brief lapse
of time before the day begins.
For a moment I have a sister, a child,
someone for whom I must be still.

ANATA

Riding the train I hold the loaf
of rye bread, still warm,
that I bought after work.
The crowds push
and I tuck it close,
soft in a paper bag.

Another time I meant to bring you
this bread, I put it above
where briefcases and hats
were supposed to go,
and letting my thoughts wander,
walked off at your station
feeling empty handed.
I turned and saw it
cooling on the rack
just as the doors shut.

But today, all day, I confess
I thought of your body—
your hips in my hands,
your hair against my shoulder,
the sound of your voice calling me
with the familiar *anata*.

Konbawa,
you say like a bell,
as I slip out of my shoes,
come into your room,
bringing with me
the smell of a kitchen.
I set the loaf down
on the kotatsu table
and you smile.

I love
what our hands say
when they feel
the warmth of our bodies,
how we'll break the bread
still fresh,
and hold each other
until morning.

WASHING THE WOK

This morning I wash the wok
then boil coffee with Guatemalan beans
I buy each week, weighed exactly on scales.
Outside the sun has evaporated
last night's bright puddles of neon.
Steam settles in cool beads on the window.

It's not enough to remember
how she left dinner early
and I followed her, how I held
a washcloth to cool her fever
and later washed the dishes, thinking
if only I could make them clean...
All summer she forgave me the peas
on my plate I would not finish.

I have counted the years, all the seasons
we ate together, against the hours
I scoured pots in the kitchen after she died.
I've learned to cook with woks,
to watch their drama as though they might
tell me something, and later to clean,
my hands in hot water—
I have not finished my grief.

THE WILLOWS OF GINZA

The willows of Ginza
that ran along the Sumida river
are gone, cleared for wider roads,
replaced by the smaller ginkgo.
Between shorn, concrete banks,
I see a boat coming downstream
in evening, strung with lanterns,
shadows hopping in the yellow
light of paper screens, the rhythm
of drum and wail of samisen strings,
a low chant calling across the water...

I remember my mother,
how once I heard her weep.
I am standing in our yard,
holding a branch of willow.
Its little buds will not
twist off easily in my hands,
when I hear her cry,
a sound I've never heard before.
All is silent, as I listen
with oak, the buckeye, and maple.

I am there in the yard,
planted deep for my mother.
I have not gone anywhere.